T0066651

WORLD'S FAVORITE SOLOS For CLASSIC GUITAR

ORIGINAL TRANSCRIPTIONS
**COMPILED AND
EDITED BY**

HARVEY VINSON

FOREWORD

The classic guitar has ascended to an "uncontested prominence in the musical galaxy", as expressed by the eminent guitarist, Andres Segovia. The recognized position of the classic guitar in to-day's music world has resulted from the devotion to the instrument and the brilliant works written for it by prominent composer-guitarists through the centuries, headed by Fernando Sor and Francioso Tarrega. Guitarists who have achieved world wide recognition have attested to the power and effectiveness of the classic guitar, like Alirio Diaz, Julian Bream and Manuel Gayol.

As the instrument gains popularity, the demand for great classic guitar compositions increases proportionately.

We are here offering an anthology of the finest works ever written for the classic guitar. These are the compositions that have been heard on the American and international concert stages time and time again.

We have included proper fingering and valid dynamic and tempo indications, conspicuously absent from many of the current editions of classic guitar music. We are indeed fortunate in having obtained an editor whose years of study at the Julliard and the Manhattan schools of music, and a wealth of experience in teaching and performing on the instrument, qualify him for this highly specialized and intricate task.

The first printings of this anthology were so well-received that a new volume: "Selected Masterpieces for the Classic Guitar" (World's Favorite Series No. 56) was added. At the suggestion of Mr. David C. Thomson of Lexington, Kentucky, both volumes have been painstakingly re-edited to improve fingerings and phrasings. It is through the help and advice of such experienced teachers as Mr. Thomson that the World's Favorite Series has gained its popularity among musicians.

**Robert Kail
Ashley Publications**

CONTENTS

CONTENTS *(Continued)*

PAVANA No. 1

LUIS MILAN
(1500-1561)

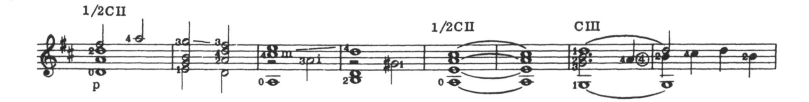

PAVANA No. 2

Andante

LUIS MILAN

PRELUDIUM

WILLIAM BYRDE
(1538-1623)

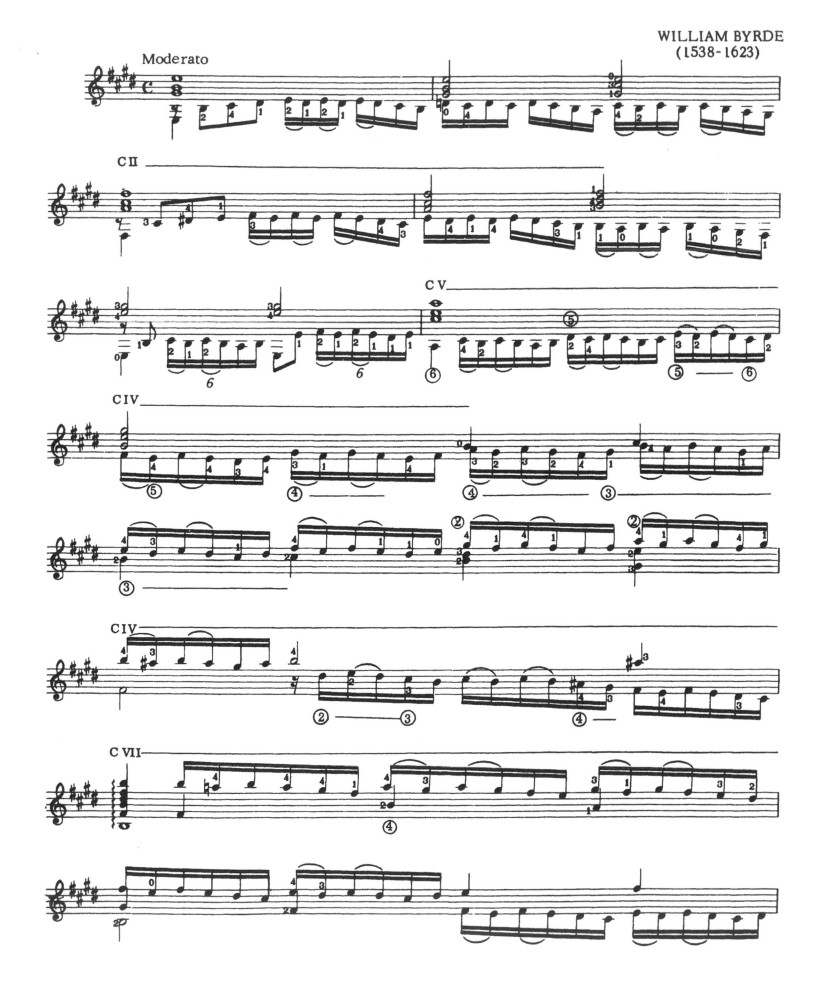

MASCHERATA

Andante

ANONYMOUS

MINUET IN D

ROBERT DE VISÉE
(17th Century)

Andantino

BOUREE

ROBERT DE VISÉE

Allegretto

MINUET IN D MINOR

ROBERT DE VISÉE

SARABANDE

ROBERT DE VISÉE

MINUET IN E MINOR

ROBERT DE VISÉE

MINUET

HENRY PURCELL
(1659-1695)

LITTLE FUGUE

DOMENICO ZIPOLI
(1675-1726)

Allegretto

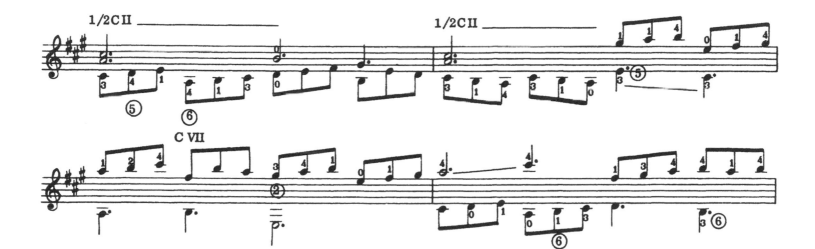

BOUREE

JOHANN SEBASTIAN BACH
(1685- 17.50)

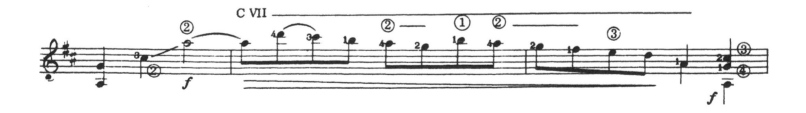

BOUREE IN E MINOR

JOHANN SEBASTIAN BACH

PRELUDE

JOHANN SEBASTIAN BACH

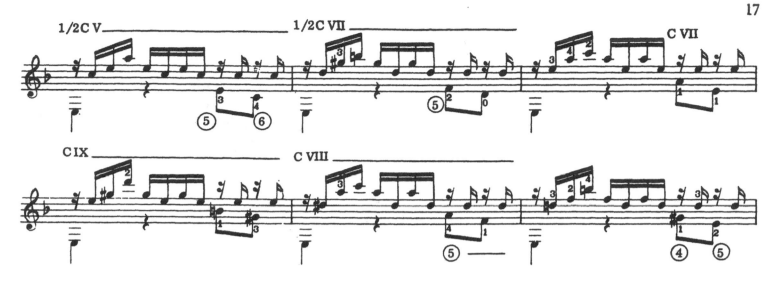

MINUET

Andantino

JOHANN SEBASTIAN BACH

ANDANTE

WOLFGANG AMADEUS MOZART
(1756-1791)

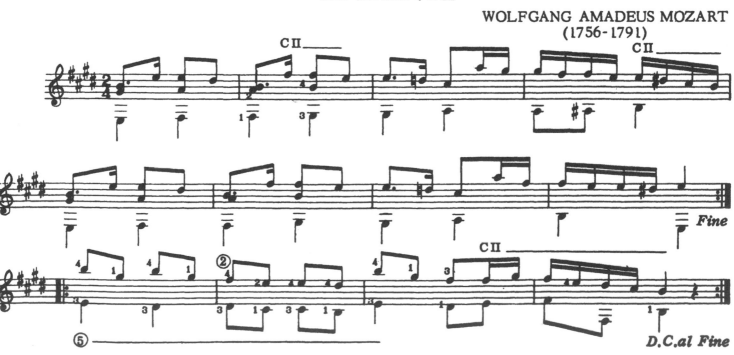

Fine

D.C. al Fine

ALLEGRETTO

FERNANDO CARULLI
(1770-1841)

Fine

D.C. al Fine

RONDO

Poco allegretto

FERNANDO CARULLI

WALTZ

Moderato

FERNANDO CARULLI

Fine

D. C. al Fine

ANDANTE

FERNANDO CARULLI

ANDANTINO

FERNANDO CARULLI

PRELUDE IN D MINOR

FRANCESCO MOLINO
(1775-1847)

PRELUDE IN E MINOR

FRANCESCO MOLINO

PRELUDE IN B FLAT

FRANCESCO MOLINO

SPANISH BALLAD

TRADITIONAL

Andante

STUDY IN C

FERNANDO SOR
(1778-1839)

STUDY IN A

FERNANDO SOR

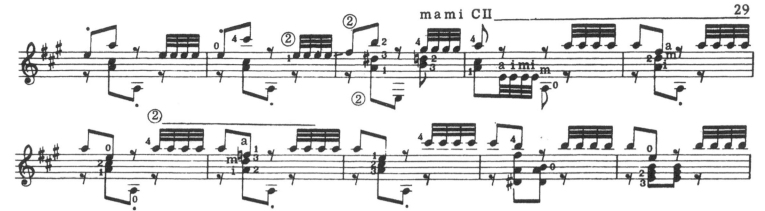

STUDY IN D

FERNANDO SOR

Moderato

STUDY IN B MINOR

FERNANDO SOR

STUDY IN A

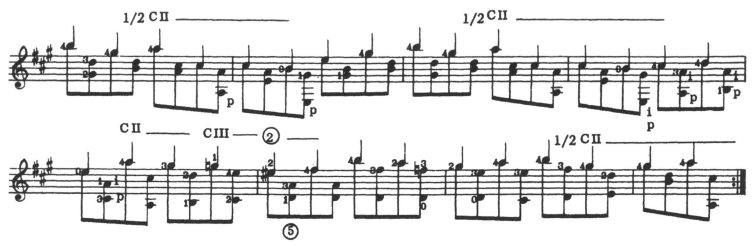

STUDY IN D

STUDY IN C

FERNANDO SOR

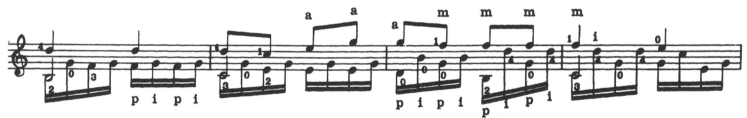

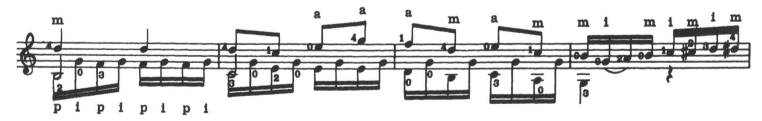

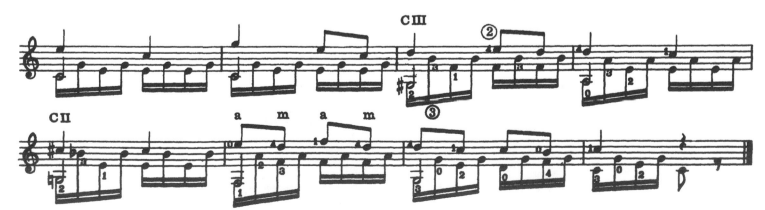

STUDY IN A MINOR

FERNANDO SOR

STUDY IN D MINOR

FERNANDO SOR

STUDY IN G

FERNANDO SOR

STUDY IN C

Allegro moderato

FERNANDO SOR

STUDY IN Bb

FERNANDO SOR

STUDY IN A

FERNANDO SOR

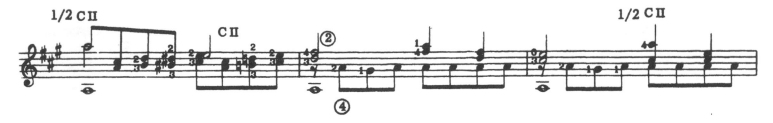

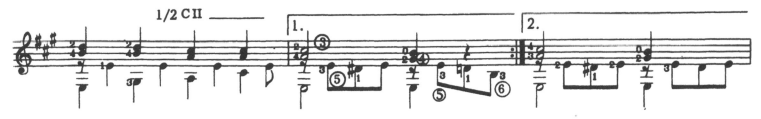

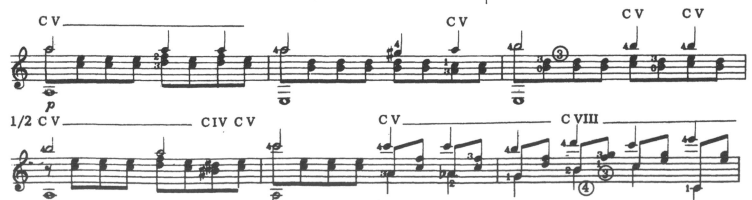

RONDO

FERNANDO SOR

Allegretto

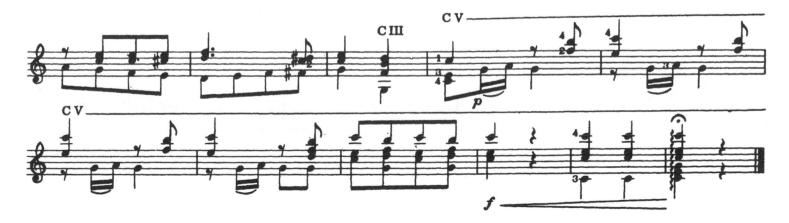

LECCION IN A MINOR

LECCION IN A

MINUET IN D

 =D

FERNANDO SOR

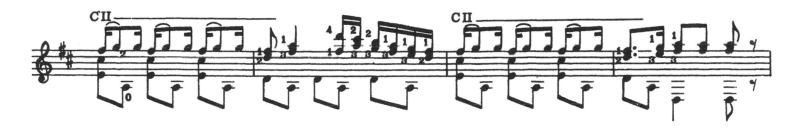

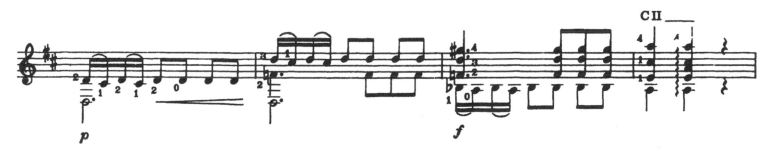

MINUET IN G

FERNANDO SOR

MINUET IN A

Andante maestoso

FERNANDO SOR

MINUET IN C

FERNANDO SOR

Allegro

Fine

D. C. al Fine

MINUET IN G

MINUET IN C

FERNANDO SOR

D. C. al Fine

VARIATION ON A THEME OF MOZART

Theme

Andante

FERNANDO SOR

First Variation
Moderato

Second Variation
Adagio (Minor)

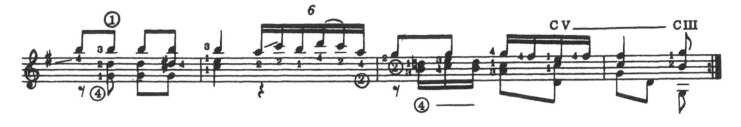

Third Variation
Moderato

Fourth Variation
Allegretto

Fifth Variation
Allegro

Sixth Variation
Presto

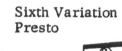

ALLEGRO

MAURO GIULIANI
(1780-1840)

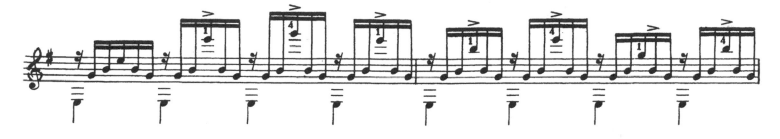

MAESTOSO

MAURO GIULIANI

ALLEGRO

MAURO GIULIANI

DANCE RONDO

MAURO GIULIANI

CADENCE

ALLEGRETTO

ANDANTINO

MAURO GIULIANI

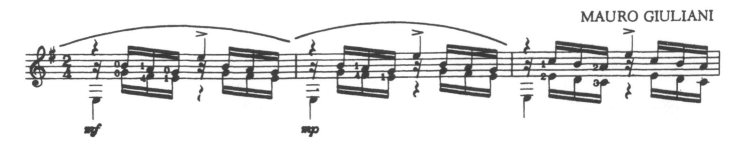

ALLEGRETTO

MAURO GIULIANI

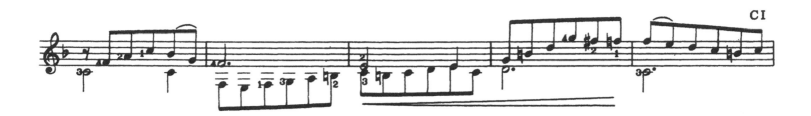

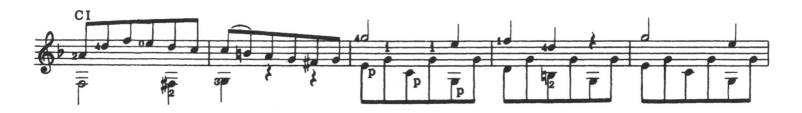

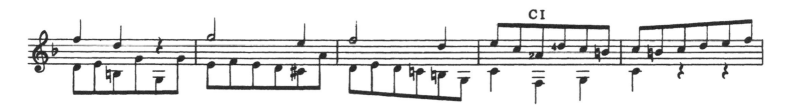

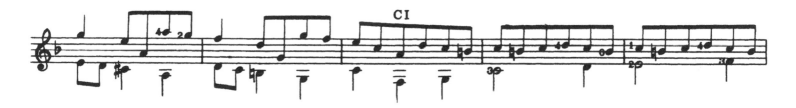

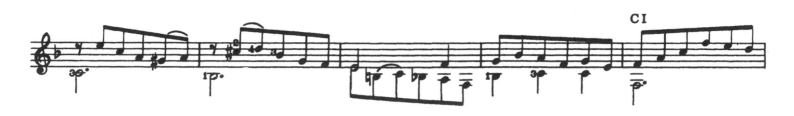

MODERATO

MAURO GIULIANI

MODERATO

MAURO GIULIANI

ALLEGRETTO

MAURO GIULIANI

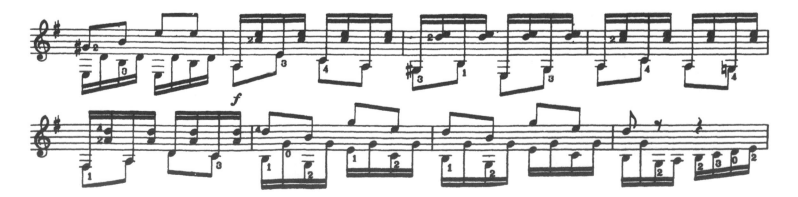

ALLEGRETTO

MAURO GIULIANI

ANDANTE

MAURO GIULIANI

PRELUDE

Allegro

DIONISIO AGUADO
(1789-1849)

ADAGIO

DIONISIO AGUADO

CAPRICE

LUIGI LEGNANI
(1790-1877)

Adagio

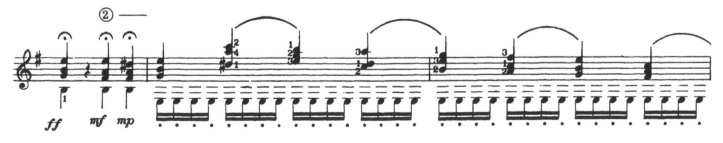

CAPRICE

LUIGI LEGNANI

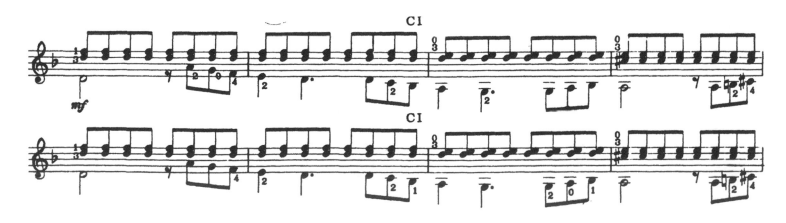

STUDY IN F

Allegretto

MATTEO CARCASSI
(1792-1853)

STUDY IN A

MATTEO CARCASSI

STUDY IN A

MATTEO CARCASSI

STUDY IN C

Allegro

MATTEO CARCASSI

STUDY IN A MINOR

MATTEO CARCASSI

STUDY IN A MINOR

MATTEO CARCASSI

STUDY IN C

Andante

MATTEO CARCASSI

ETUDE

NAPOLEON COSTE
(1806-1883)

ETUDE

ETUDE

NAPOLEON COSTE

ETUDE

NAPOLEON COSTE

PRELUDE

NAPOLEON COSTE

BAGATELLE

Moderato

ROBERT ALEXANDER SCHUMANN
(1810-1856)

MELODY

ROBERT SCHUMANN

RECUERDOS DE LA ALHAMBRA

FRANCISCO TARREGA
(1854-1909)

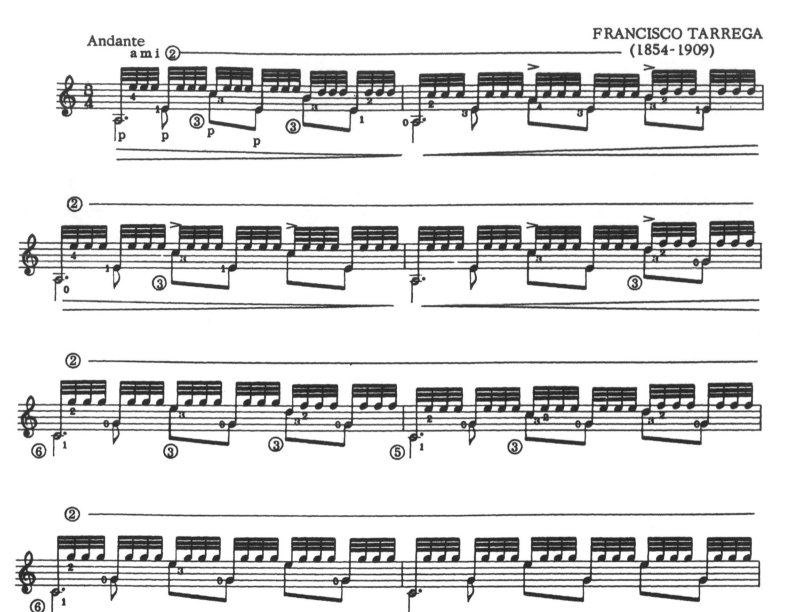

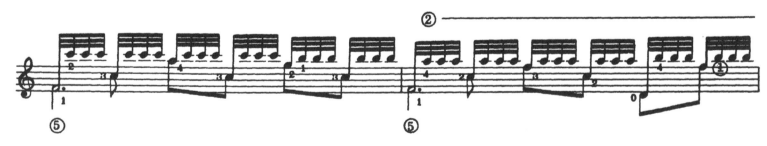

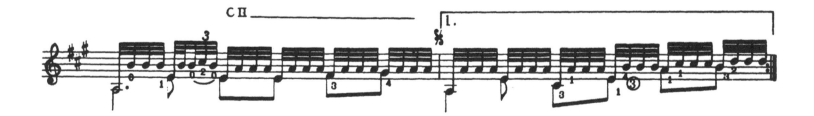

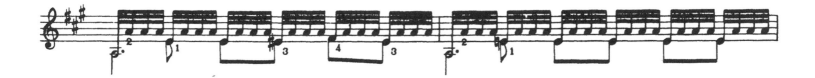

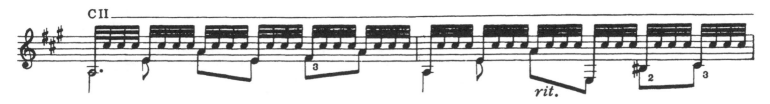

CAPRICHO ARABE

FRANCISCO TARREGA

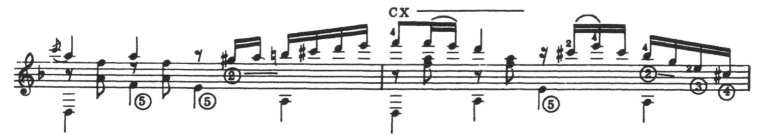

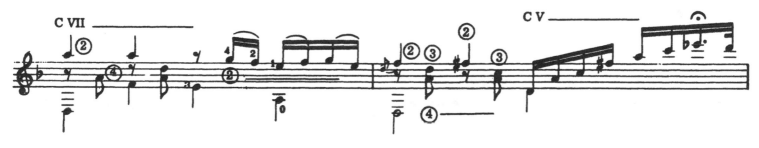

a tempo

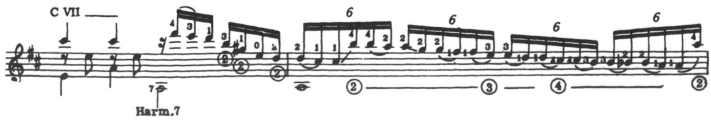

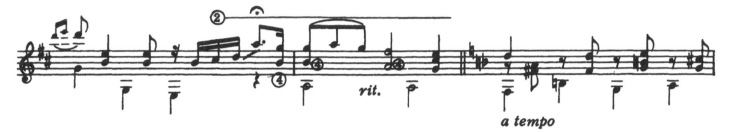

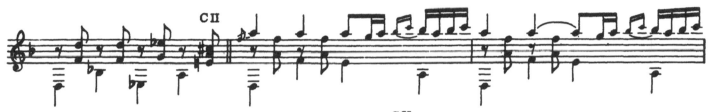

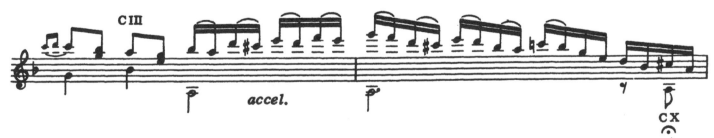

LAGRIMA

Largo

FRANCISCO TARREGA

MAZURCA

FRANCISCO TARREGA

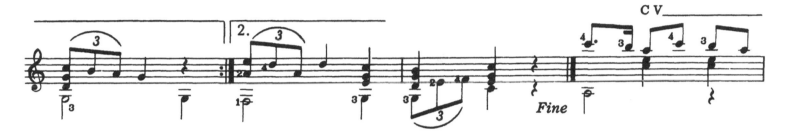

Fine

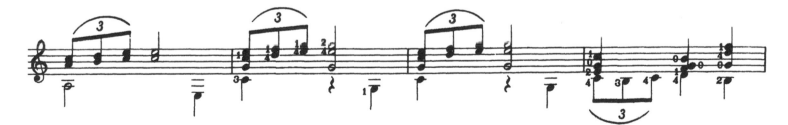

D. C. al Fine

PAVANA

FRANCISCO TARREGA

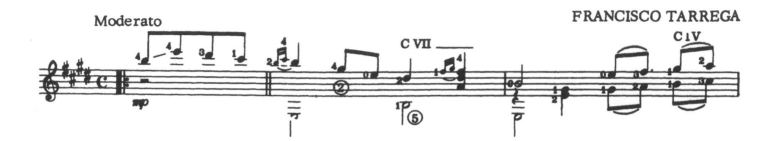

ADELITA

FRANCISCO TARREGA

MARIA

FRANCISCO TARREGA

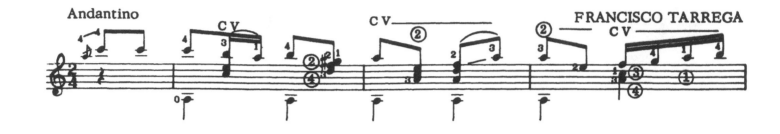

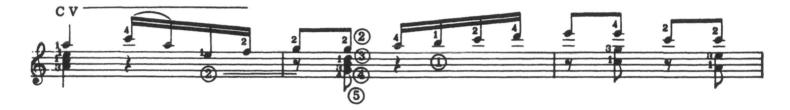

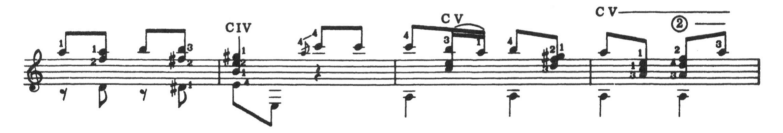

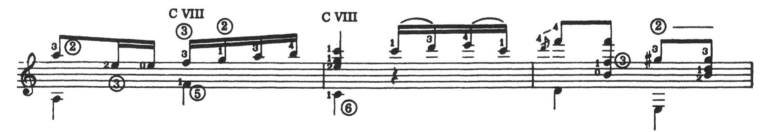

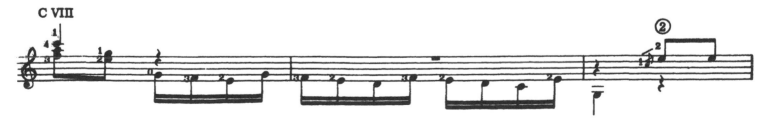

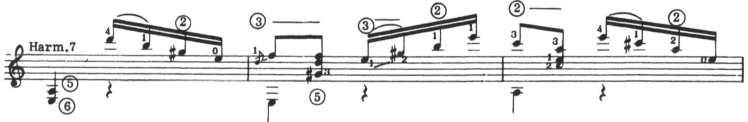

PRELUDE

Andante sostenuto

FRANCISCO TARREGA

PRELUDE

FRANCISCO TARREGA

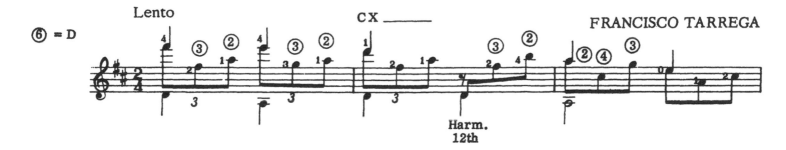

PRELUDE

FRANCISCO TARREGA

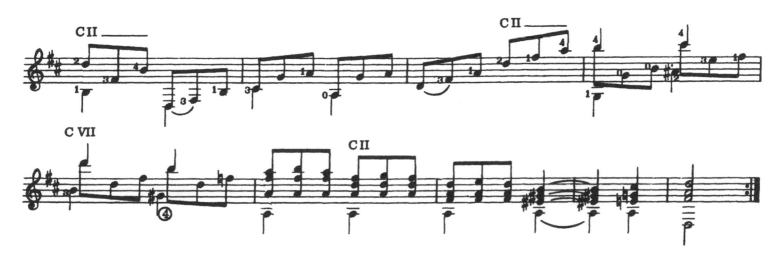

MARIETA

FRANCISCO TARREGA

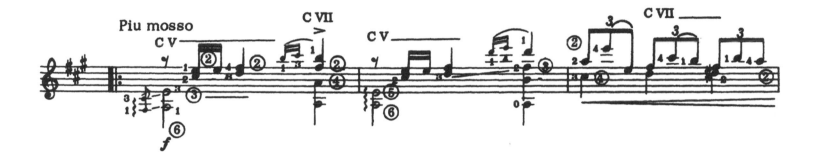

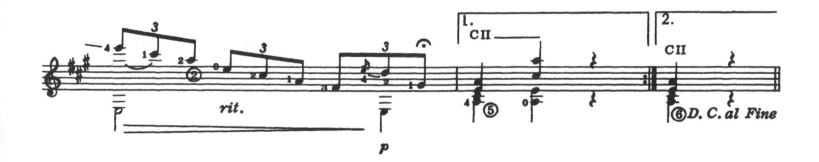

LEYENDA

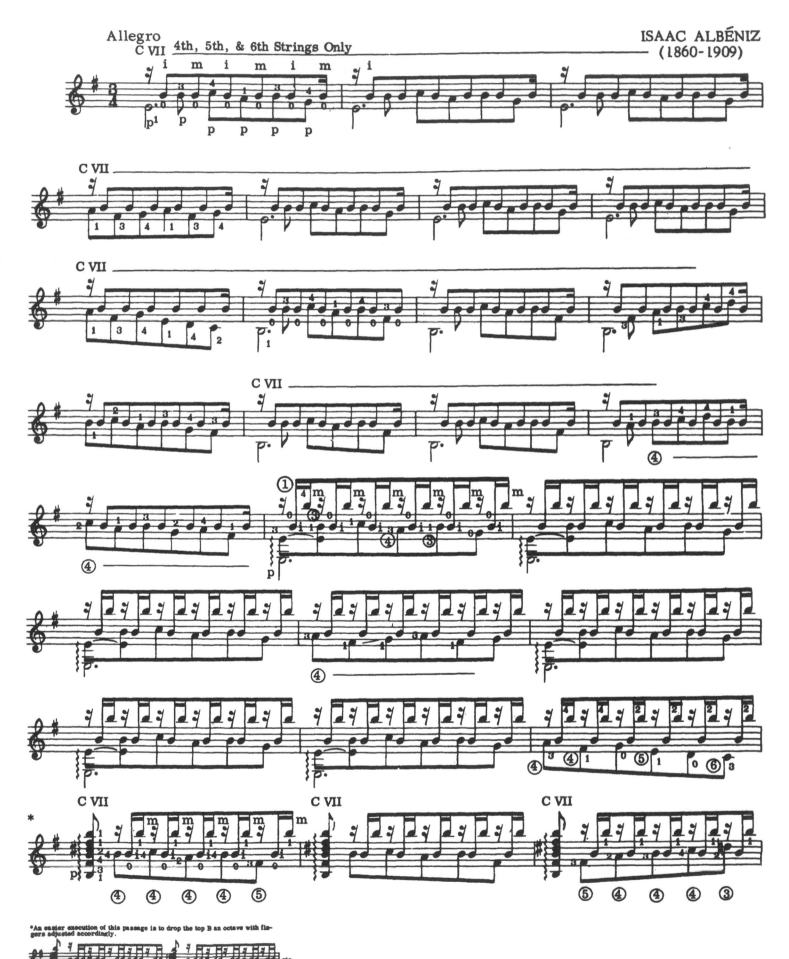

*An easier execution of this passage is to drop the top B an octave with fingers adjusted accordingly.

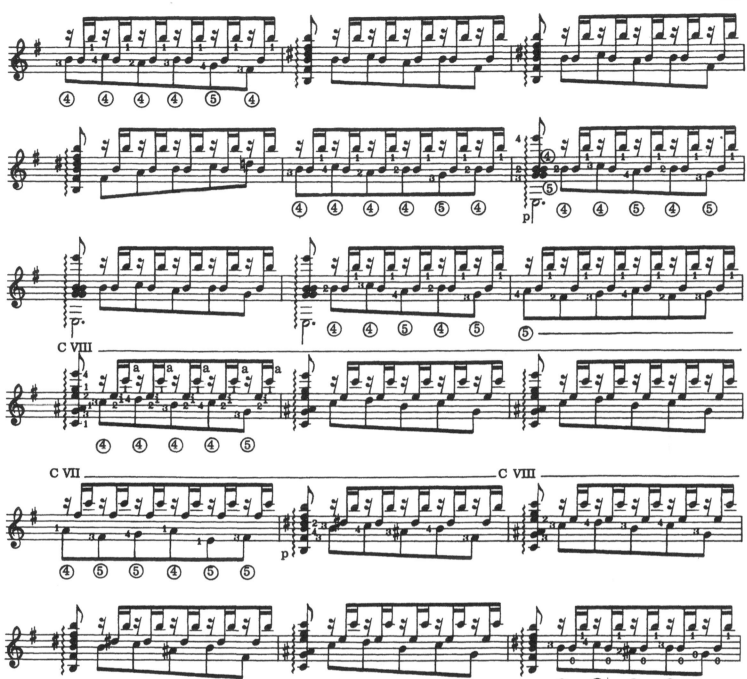

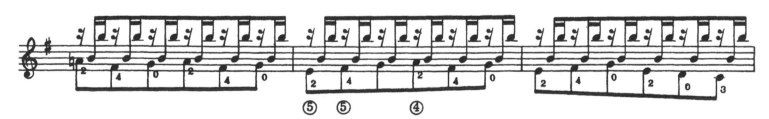

NOCTURNE DE SALON

Guitar One

Guitar One

FERNANDO CARULLI
(1770-1841)

NOCTURNE DE SALON

Guitar Two

Guitar Two

FERNANDO CARULLI
(1770-1841)

Allegro

Guitar One

Guitar Two

Guitar Two

Larghetto

Guitar One

Guitar Two

Allegro

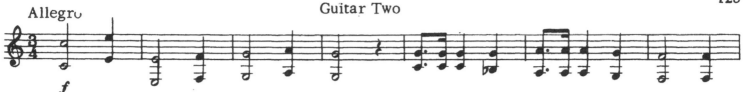

Guitar One

Guitar Two